The Best of Character

BULLETIN BOARD IDEAS

SONG TITLES

The Best of Character

It has been said that to live is to teach. *The Best of Character* is dedicated to the many teaching and administrative colleagues with whom I have had the privilege to work during my more than 30 years in public education. These colleagues have lived and taught by example.

The individuals include such mentors as Drs. Bernard McKenzie, Gary Weesner, William Christopher, Fred Bechtold, H. Dean Evans, Mr. Bill McColly, Mr. Otis Archey, Mr. Paul Davis, and my doctoral program advisor and friend: Dr. Orval Conner, professor emeritus of Miami University in Oxford, Ohio.

Other colleagues and persons who have enriched my life by exemplifying moral virtue through good teaching examples are the late Quaker theologian, author, professor and scholar, Dr. D. Elton Trueblood, Drs. Suellen Reed, Evelyn Holt-Otten, Tim Jackson, Steve Barone, Dan Jeran, Duane Hoak, Gordon Mendenhall, Phil Vincent, Ms. Caroline Hanna, Mr. Charles Hilton, Mr. Bill Gavaghen, Mrs. Barbara Stryker, Mrs. Susan Jordan, Mr. Ron Davie, Mr. Dan Fitzgibbon, Elaine and Pat O'pelt, Jean and George Davis, Mr. Phil Farr, Mr. Don Peslis, Mary Ellen Hamer, Mrs. Cheryl McLaughlin, and pastors Sam Stone and Stan Banker.

Since our character, as Aristotle states, is living "the life of right conduct," I would be remiss in not expressing my gratitude to my parents, Everett and Ellie Hodgin, and my mother-in-law, Velma Armacost, all of whom have lived the life of right conduct for more than eighty years. I am grateful to my wife and friend, Sandi, who has constantly encouraged and challenged me to examine myself, my motivations and my moral benchmarks.

Finally, I dedicate this resource to my children, Stephen and Annemarie, who helped to teach me the importance of faith, moral wisdom, courage and perseverance. And to our granddaughters Kaitlyn Marie and Emma Jayne who I hope will grow to become morally responsible children and adults.

To the above named mentors, colleagues, friends, family members and others too numerous to mention, I write this book as both an appreciation and affirmation of the difference you have made in my life, a difference that causes me to strive to become what I am morally capable of becoming.

I would like to acknowledge the many dedicated teachers, administrators, support staff and the Board of Education in the Metropolitan School District of Lawrence Township, Indianapolis, Indiana, who recognize that character education is both a "message" and a "mission" in which each of us accepts our role as character educators for all students by design rather than by default.

And to Linda Knoderer, my long-time administrative assistant, whose dedicated support, balanced perspective and advice are greatly valued. Special appreciation is extended to my daughter, Annemarie Williams, who devoted hours to typing and critiquing the manuscript.

This book is intended for use by teachers (K-12), school counselors and administrators. The quotes on character, the teaching activities and bulletin board ideas are practical, applicable and easy to use or modify.

Former President Theodore Roosevelt once said, "To educate a person in mind and not in morals is to educate a menace to society," while America's 16th president Abraham Lincoln wrote, "The philosophy and morals taught in the schoolhouse today will be the philosophy and morals practiced by the next generation's government." How prophetic is the wisdom of these great Americans who themselves modeled lives of virtue and noble character.

As responsible and caring educators, we are in a privileged position to help "stem the tide of moral malaise and mediocrity," for as Lincoln recognized, it is the schoolhouse where we have the opportunity and the expectation to teach virtuous principles and moral behaviors. While we are only part of the "character equation," with the home, community and businesses comprising the other essential factors, as educators we have the "power and the possibility" to help re-direct our nation's moral compass and our society's well being. The future of our democracy depends on what we do or what we choose not to do with our role as character educators.

Kevin Ryan, former Director of the Center for the Advancement of Ethics at Boston University said, "Character Education is not the school's newest fad, rather it is the school's oldest mission." It provides the foundation for academic learning and moral thinking, being and doing. Character education must become a deliberate effort in our homes, schools and communities by which we come to recognize as the late Dr. Norman Vincent Peale did when he wrote, "The world is desperately in need of men and women of character who have the courage to do the right things about wrong conditions."

The quotes, activities, and ideas contained in this book can help educators deliberately plan a variety of character education activities. These activities capitalize on the daily "teachable moments" (or "character moments") we encounter as well as utilize teachers' creative resources to integrate the information into daily lessons and various classroom activities. It is hoped that principals and teachers will use the materials to help enhance the "moral ethos and climate of the school." Nationally renowned character educator and author Dr. Thomas Lickona believes that, "Character education creates the climate for learning and caring in schools."

Following are some specific ideas for use of this book:

- Read or have students read character quotes as part of the daily/morning announcements. There are enough quotes included for each character trait for you to use a different one each school day of the month you are emphasizing that trait.
- When working with younger children, paraphrase quotes so children can understand their true meaning.
- Post character quotes on the school Web site.
- Print character quotes in teacher and school newsletters.
- Use character quotes for student writing assignments and journals.
- Use character quotes for teacher/student discussion.
- Apply character quotes as computer screensavers.
- Encourage students to write their own character quotes, poems, bumper stickers, songs or raps.
- Decorate bulletin boards or chalkboards with character themes. Included bulletin board ideas may be enlarged and used as posters, bulletin boards, handouts or coloring sheets. The bulletin board ideas can be modified for different grade levels.
- Have students use a variety of quotes and create a character message or story.
- Have students do reports about the famous individuals who are quoted in this book and tell what dominate character traits or virtues these individuals demonstrated in their lives.
- Create a "Character Quote Collage" and ask students to bring drawings or pictures from magazines to illustrate the quotes.
- Use related character activities to help students internalize the character traits.
- Encourage students to write their own or a classroom/school "character pledge".
- Play the suggested songs and ask students to discuss the character traits represented in each. Ask students to suggest other songs with character/moral messages.

It is my hope that you, your students and your school will benefit from the information provided and that you will recognize that effective character education is not a program nor a prescription rather it is a continuous and deliberate process and practice of expecting students to "know the good", "love the good" and have the courage to "do the right thing." May you go forth with the enthusiasm and commitment that is reflected in the wisdom of the great scholar and writer Ralph Waldo Emerson: "People of character are the conscience of society."

"Character education is about the connection of the Head, the Heart, and the Hand which encourages civility, service to others and moral thinking and behaving."

— Duane Hodgin

Duane Hodgin, Ph.D. is the Assistant Superintendent for Educational Support Services for the Metropolitan School District of Lawrence Township in Indianapolis, Indiana. He has served in various teaching and administrative levels for more than three decades.

Throughout his career, he has received numerous educational awards, recognitions and citations. Dr. Hodgin coordinates the district's "Caring About Character" (K-12) character education initiative. He has written and had published numerous articles for newspapers and journals.

Dr. Hodgin now serves as a character educator and school safety specialist speaker, trainer and presenter for the Indiana Department of Education, the Indiana Principals Leadership Academy and the Indiana School Safety Specialist Academy. He has presented at numerous local, state, regional and national character education conferences as well as conducting training and in-service workshops for schools and school districts in Indiana and throughout the country. He was instrumental in working with Indiana's Governor Frank O'Bannon and staff to help plan and establish the Indiana Center for Character Development at Anderson University in Anderson, Indiana. He now serves on the Advisory Board for the Center and is a primary trainer/facilitator for the Center.

Duane's wife, Sandi, is an Assistant to the Principal at Lawrence Township's Brook Park Talent Development Academy. The National Character Education Partnership (CEP) recognized the school in 1999-2000 as a School of Excellence, one of only 21 schools nationwide.

For information on character education in-service/workshops
or keynote speeches, please contact:
Duane Hodgin
(317) 423-8310 or (317) 577-4021
dhodgin@msdlt.k12.in.us

Quotations

"Choose your thoughts with care, and let all your words be kind."

— Anonymous

Compassion is the chief love
of human existence.
— *Fyodor Dostoyevsky*

A kind and compassionate act
is often its own reward.
— *William Bennett*

Caring is an attitude to God himself.
— *William Shakespeare*

Kind words can be short and easy to speak,
but their echoes are endless.
— *Mother Teresa*

Kindness is the golden chain by which
society is bound together.
— *Johann Goethe*

"**Kindness is the language with which the deaf can hear and the blind can see.**"

— **Mark Twain**

No act of kindness, however small, goes unnoticed.
— *Aesop*

Kindness is being able to imagine as one's own the suffering and joy of others.
— *André Gide*

We are made kind by being kind.
— *Eric Hoffer*

If you stop to be kind, you must swerve often from your path.
— *Helen Webb*

Wise sayings often fall on barren ground; but a kind word is never thrown away.
— *Sir Arthur Hedges*

"Treat men greatly and they will show themselves to be great."

— Ralph Waldo Emerson

The best portion of a good person's life are the little, nameless, unremembered acts of kindness and love.
— *Anonymous*

Caring is nobility's true badge.
— *William Shakespeare*

Caring is the sunshine in which virtue grows.
— *Robert Ingersoll*

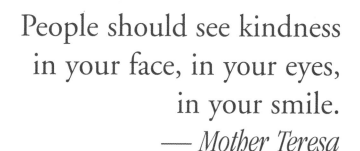

People should see kindness in your face, in your eyes, in your smile.
— *Mother Teresa*

"A good head and a good heart are always a formidable combination."

— Nelson Mandela

Kindness is the better part of goodness.
— *William Somerset Maugham*

Kindness makes one feel good whether it's being done to you or by you.
— *Anonymous*

You cannot do a kindness too soon, because you never know how soon it will be too late.
— *Anonymous*

The power of love and caring can change the world.
— *James Autry*

The kindest people are those who forgive and forget.
— *Anonymous*

"To handle yourself, use your head; to handle others, use your heart."

— Anonymous

The ideas that have lighted my way
have been kindness, beauty and truth.
— *Albert Schweitzer*

If you must experience, why
not experience caring.
— *Anonymous*

May we learn to feel another's woe.
— *Alexander Pope*

Those who bring sunshine to the lives
of others cannot keep it from themselves.
— *James Barrie*

Let your face radiate kindness and
a positive attitude; smile a lot.
— *Dainer Forrest*

"It's not within everyone's power to be beautiful, but we can make sure that the words that come out of our mouths are."

— Anonymous

Kindness gives birth to kindness.
— *Sophocles*

There is no better exercise
for the heart than reaching down
and lifting others up.
— *John Andrew Holmes*

Always do these things: Show mercy to others, be kind, humble, gentle and patient.
— *St. Paul*

If you love the people who are in your own family, then love will go out to everyone.
— *Mother Teresa*

"HELPING OTHERS MAKES OUR HEART STRONG."

— ANONYMOUS

I expect to pass through this life
but once. If therefore, there be any
kindness I can show or any good
I can do to any fellow being, let me
do it now and not neglect it, as
I shall not pass this way again.
— *William Penn*

With malice toward none,
with charity for all.
— *Abraham Lincoln*

If you care for yourself,
you can care for others too.
— *Paul Tillich*

Kind words cost little
but accomplish much.
— *Hal Urban*

"Be kind, for everyone you meet is fighting a battle."

— Plato

Kindness in words creates confidence; kindness in thinking creates profoundness; kindness in giving creates love.
— *Lao-Tzu*

I try not to let my mouth say anything that my head cannot stand.
— *Louis Armstrong*

The people who truly make the most difference in our lives are those who truly care.
— *Anonymous*

Whenever there is another person, there is an opportunity for kindness.
— *Seneca*

Caring is a gift
of the soul.

From a little spark of kindness
may burst a mighty flame.

The key words in character
are "care" and "act".

Small acts of kindness
can create large feelings of joy.

Kindness is able to accomplish
what anger cannot.

Quotations from the Author

"Our citizenship in the United States is our national character."

— Thomas Paine

It is not the function of our Government to keep the citizen from falling into error; it is the function of the citizen to keep the Government from falling into error.
— Robert Jackson

I only regret that I have but one life to lose for my country.
— Nathan Hale

The laws of necessity, of self-preservation, of saving our country when in danger is the highest of obligations.
— Thomas Jefferson

When a nation is filled with strife, then do patriots flourish.
—Lao Tzu

CITIZENSHIP & PATRIOTISM

Quotations

"Ask not what your country can do for you — ask what you can do for your country."

— John F. Kennedy

The first requisite of a good citizen in our country is that he shall be able and willing to pull his own weight.
— *Theodore Roosevelt*

Where freedom rings, there is my country.
— *Anonymous*

It is the duty of all wise, free and virtuous governments to encourage virtue.
— *John Jay*

Patriotism is the same as the love of humanity.
— *Mohatma Ghandi*

The fate of an empire depends upon the moral education of its youth.

Aristotle

Character is the only secure foundation of the state.
— *Calvin Coolidge*

It is our character that supports the premise of our future — far more than particular government programs or policies.
— *William Bennett*

The true test of civilization is the kind of person the country turns out.
— *Ralph Waldo Emerson*

The central purpose of a society, understood as a moral community, is the cultivation of virtue.
— *Amitai Etzioni*

"The worth of the state in the long run is the worth of the individual composing it."

— John Stuart Mills

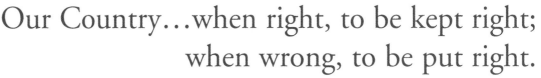

If I have added to the pride of America, I am happy.
— *Carl Sandburg*

Our Country…when right, to be kept right; when wrong, to be put right.
— *Carl Schurz*

Let us have faith that might makes. Right makes might, and in that faith, let us, to the end dare to do our duty as we understand it.
— *Abraham Lincoln*

Our children should be vaccinated and revaccinated with the Bill of Rights and its meaning.
— *H. Ross Perot*

"THE PURPOSE OF FREEDOM IS TO CREATE IT FOR OTHERS."

— BERNARD MALOMUD

One thing I know: the only ones among you who will be really happy are those who will have sought and found how to serve.
— *Albert Schweitzer*

The truest friend to the liberty of this country is he who tries to promote its virtue.
— *Samuel Adams*

Patriotism, to be truly American, begins with human allegiance.
— *Norman Cousins*

The foundations of our national policy will be laid on the pure and immutable principles of private morality.
— *George Washington*

"A virtuous citizen is indispensable to the preservation of our democracy."

— James Madison

The promotion of virtue requires
a strong government, strong enough
to be able to help people deny themselves,
restrain themselves against their desires.
— *George Will*

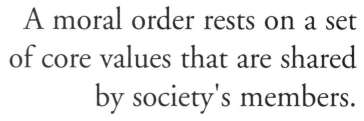

A moral order rests on a set
of core values that are shared
by society's members.
— *Amitai Etzioni*

There is no substitute for
hard work and effort
beyond the call of mere duty.
That is what strengthens
the soul and enables one's character.
— *Walter Camp*

Duty, service and honor
of country are dependent
upon people of character.

A true patriot is recognized
by his conscience of character.

Citizenship is both
a privilege and responsibility
that requires people
to do what is right
because it is the right thing to do.

Quotations from the Author

"Courage is resistance to fear, mastery of fear – not absence of fear."

— Mark Twain

Courage is grace under pressure.
— *Ernest Hemingway*

Courage without conscience
is a wild beast.
— *Robert Ingersoll*

Courage is not simply one of the virtues
but the form of every virtue at its testing point.
— *C.S. Lewis*

Life shrinks or expands
in proportion to one's courage.
— *Anais Nin*

Stand up for what is right
even if you stand alone.
— *Anonymous*

COURAGE

Quotations

"In any moment of decision, the best thing you can do is the right thing."

— Theodore Roosevelt

The ultimate measure of a man is not where he stands in moments of comfort and convenience, but where he stands in times of challenge and controversy.
— *Dr. Martin Luther King, Jr.*

It takes great courage to faithfully follow what we know to be true.
— *Sara Anderson*

It is not in the still calm of life that great character is formed, rather great necessities call out our great virtues.
— *Abagail Adams*

To seek what is right and not to do it is lack of courage.
— *Confucius*

"What everyone else is doing is quite irrelevant when it comes to doing what is right."
— Russell Gough

Standing for what is right when it is unpopular is the true test of moral character.
— *Margaret Chase Smith*

The world is desperately in need of men and women who have the courage to do the right thing about wrong conditions.
— *Dr. Norman Vincent Peale*

You will never do anything in this world without courage. It is the greatest quality of the mind next to honor.
— *James Allen*

Courage is the quality which guarantees all others.
— *Winston Churchill*

"Courage is not freedom from fear; it is being afraid and going on."
— Anonymous

Courage is the integrity of strength
that causes one to overcome tragedy.
— *Eugene Brussell*

Courage is doing what you are afraid to do.
There can be no courage unless you are afraid.
— *Eddie Rickenbucker*

Stand with any man when he is right,
and part from him when he is wrong.
— *Abraham Lincoln*

Courage is being the only one
who knows you are afraid.
— *Anonymous*

"The courage to speak must be matched by the wisdom to listen."

— Anonymous

Courage is not the absence of fear, but the conquest of it.
— *Anonymous*

Tell a man he is brave, and you help him to become so.
— *Thomas Carlyle*

Courage is that which compels you to do the thing you think you cannot do.
— *Anonymous*

Our character is challenged in the river of life where there are strong currents while, left unchallenged, carry us downstream.
— *Kurt Bruner*

"IF YOU DON'T STAND FOR SOMETHING, YOU WILL FALL FOR EVERYTHING."

— ANONYMOUS

Courage is the perfect sensibility of the measure of danger and a willingness to endure it.
— *General William Sherman*

All progress has resulted from people who took unpopular positions.
— *Adali Stevenson*

Faced with a crisis, the man of character falls back upon himself.
— *Charles De Gaulle*

Character isn't about doing what you have a right to do, but about doing what is right.
— *John Nabers*

"To accept responsibility for a mistake takes true courage."

— Anonymous

It is not because things
are difficult that we do not dare;
it is because we do not dare
that they are difficult.
— *Seneca*

Why is it that my people can
demonstrate physical courage
but struggle when it comes
to demonstrating moral courage?
— *Mark Twain*

It takes desire to be a person
of character; it takes courage
to demonstrate it.

The strength of our character
is in direct proportion to
our willingness to demonstrate
the courage to do the right thing.

To stand alone for what is right
is one of life's most noble deeds.

"Manners are the happy way of doing things."

— Ralph Waldo Emerson

Manners are more important than laws.
— *Edmund Burke*

If good manners were an animal, it would be an endangered species.
— *Henry Rogers*

To make good manners ring true, one must feel them, not merely exhibit them.
—*Amy Vanderbilt*

Never underestimate the power of simple courtesy. Your courtesy may not be returned or remembered, but discourtesy will.
— *Princess Jackson Smith*

Politeness is the chief sign of culture.
— *Balastar Gracian*

"Treat your superior as a father, your equal as a brother, and your inferior as a son."

— Persian Proverb

Good manners are an impassible wall of defense.
— *Ralph Waldo Emerson*

Self-respect is at the bottom line of all good manners.
— *Edward Martin*

Manners is simply the practice of expressing consideration for the feelings of others.
— *Alice Miller*

The great secret is having the same manners for all human souls.
— *George Bernard Shaw*

Politeness shows hope and trust in men.
— *Henry David Thoreau*

"Manners is the art of choosing among your thoughts and behaviors."

— **Anonymous**

Manners are the final and
perfect flower of noble character.
— *William Waiter*

Good manners are made up
of small sacrifices.
— *Ralph Waldo Emerson*

A person becomes known by his manners.
— *Anonymous*

Politeness is good manners
regulated by good sense.
— *Sydney Smith*

Good manners need the support
of good manners in others.
— *Ralph Waldo Emerson*

"Rudeness is the weak man's imitation of strength."

— Eric Hoffer

There is not a single outward mark of courtesy that does not have a deep moral base.
— *Goethe*

Good manners means behaving yourself a little better than is absolutely necessary.
— *Will Cuppy*

What is courtesy? Consideration for others.
— *Mark Twain*

There can be no defense like elaborate courtesy.
— *E.V. Lucas*

Quotations

"He *who sows courtesy reaps friendship, and he who plants kindness gathers love.*"

— St. Basil

Politeness is the art of choosing among one's real thoughts.
— *Abel Stevens*

Really big people are, above everything else, courteous, considerate and generous — not just to some people in some circumstances — but to everyone all the time.
— *Thomas J. Watson*

Nothing is ever lost by courtesy. It is the cheapest of the pleasures; costs nothing and conveys much. It pleases him who gives and him who receives, and thus, like mercy, it is twice blessed.
— *Erastus Wiman*

The greater the manners,
the greater the man.

One's manners can be
a mirror of the soul.

Courtesy, like strong character,
is contagious.

Good manners is
good character in action.

"Honesty is your truest friend no matter what the circumstance."

— Abraham Lincoln

Truth alleviates rather than hurts and will always bear up against falsehood.
— *Miguel De Caravantes*

Truth is man's staff in his voyage through life.
— *Remy De Gourmont*

Truth can stand by itself.
— *Thomas Jefferson*

Truth is the most valuable thing we have.
— *Mark Twain*

Nothing astonishes men so much as common sense and honesty.
— *Ralph Waldo Emerson*

"The noblest work of God is an honest man."

— Abraham Lincoln

Honesty is telling other people the truth; integrity is telling yourself the truth.
— *Spencer Johnson*

No legacy is as rich as honesty.
— *William Shakespeare*

Honesty is the first chapter in the book of wisdom.
— *Thomas Jefferson*

Truth is a hard master and costly to serve, but it simplifies all matters.
— *Ellis Peters*

Truth has no special time of its own; its time is now — always.
—*Albert Schweitzer*

"Honesty is one thing for which there is no known substitute."

— Anonymous

Honesty is the moral conscience of the great.
— *William D'Avenant*

Without courage there cannot be truth,
and without truth, there can be
no other virtues.
— *Sir Walter Scott*

Honesty is the ability
to resist small temptations.
— *John Ciardi*

Truth is the heart of morality.
— *Thomas Henry Huxley*

Honesty is the highest thing
that man may keep.
— *Geoffrey Chaucer*

"To be persuasive, we must be believable; to be believable, we must be credible; to be credible, we must be truthful."

— Ralph Waldo Emerson

Truth never changes a cause that is just.
— *Mohatma Ghandi*

Truth is tough.
— *Oscar Wendall Holmes*

The person who is honest does not have to worry about a faulty memory.
— *Anonymous*

Truth often hurts, but it's the lie that leaves the scar.
— *Anonymous*

When truth stands in your way, it's time to change direction.
— *Anonymous*

"TRUTH IS STUBBORN; IT DOESN'T APOLOGIZE TO ANYBODY."

— ANONYMOUS

Truth is the torch
that gleams through the fog.
— *Anonymous*

When in doubt, tell the truth.
— *Mark Twain*

Honesty is the best policy.
— *George Washington*

Honesty is not always popular,
but it is always right.
— *Oscar Arias*

If you add to the truth,
you subtract from it.
— *Anonymous*

When we can be honest with ourselves,
our personal journey begins.

If honesty is the best policy,
it must also be the best practice.

Honesty, with oneself and others,
is the foundation of all virtues.

National Center for Youth Issues • Home of STARS • www.ncyi.org

"If we do not maintain justice, justice will not maintain us."

— Francis Bacon

Justice begins with the recognition of the necessity of sharing.
— *Elias Canetti*

Justice consists of doing no injury to others.
— *Cicero*

Justice must always question itself.
— *Michael Foucault*

Justice is the first requisite of civilization.
— *Sigmund Freud*

Justice is the conscience of the whole of humanity.
— *Alexander Solzhenitaryn*

"It is not who is right but what is right that is of importance."

— Thomas Huxley

Justice is the only true principle for mankind.
— *Henry Amiel*

Justice is the great standing policy of a civil society.
— *Edmund Burke*

Justice is truth in action.
— *Benjamin Disraeli*

Justice is taking from no man what is his.
— *Thomas Hobbs*

Justice is the sum of all moral duty.
— *William Godwin*

"Justice is a virtue of the soul distributing that which each person deserves."

— Diogenes Laertius

Every virtue is included in the idea and practice of justice.
— *Theognis*

Justice is best demonstrated by the heart and spirit of those who resist power over others.
— *Woodrow Wilson*

Justice is better than chivalry if we cannot have both.
— *Alice Stone Blackwell*

The foundation of justice is good faith.
— *Marcus T. Cicero*

Nothing is to be preferred before justice.
— *Socrates*

"Between friends there is no need of justice."

— Aristotle

The rain ... falls upon
the just and the unjust alike.
— *Mark Twain*

The probability that we may fail
in the struggle ought not to deter us
from the support of a cause
we believe to be just.
— *Abraham Lincoln*

Justice, not the majority,
should rule.
— *C. N. Bovee*

No man is above the law
and no man below it.
— *Theodore Roosevelt*

"The administration of justice is the firmest pillar of government."

— George Washington

Justice is a machine that,
when someone has given
it a starting push, rolls on of itself.
— *Galsworthy*

I am the inferior of any man
whose rights I trample underfoot.
— *Horace Greeley*

Injustice anywhere
is a threat to justice everywhere.
— *Dr. Martin Luther King, Jr.*

There is no wrong time
to do the right thing.
— *Anonymous*

Life is not always fair,
but we can always choose
to be fair and just.

People of character will never
compromise the justice of others.

Fairness is never guaranteed,
but a person of character
will never fail to grant it.

46

"Patience is the hardest victory."

— Aristotle

The highest stage in moral culture is when we recognize that we ought to control our thoughts.
— *Charles Darwin*

Patience is the blending of moral courage with physical timidity.
— *Thomas Harding*

Patience is full power and command of myself.
— *Ralelais*

Patience is wisdom's root.
— *Robert Burns*

He that would govern others, first must master himself.
— *Philip Massinger*

PATIENCE & SELF-CONTROL

Quotations

"PATIENCE IS OFTEN BITTER, BUT ITS FRUIT IS SWEET."

— ANONYMOUS

Patience is a reality of the heart that can be greatly enhanced with different practices.
— *Richard Carlson*

Self-control is the presence of mind in untried emergencies.
— *James Russell Lowell*

True patience means waiting without worrying.
— *Anonymous*

Patience is the best remedy for every trouble.
— *Plautus*

Patience is the greatest of all life's shock absorbers.
— *Anonymous*

"Be patient with the faults of others; they may have to be patient with yours."

— Anonymous

Patience helps one to keep things in perspective.
— *Richard Carlson*

Patience is the ability to count down before blasting off.
— *Anonymous*

Be patient. You get the chicken by hatching the egg — not by smashing it open.
— *Anonymous*

To enjoy freedom we have to control ourselves.
— *Virginia Woolf*

Have patience in all things, but mainly have patience in yourself.
— *St. Frances de Sales*

"He is a fool who cannot get angry, but he is a wise man who will not."

— Anonymous

Patience adds a dimension of ease and acceptance to one's life. It is essentially inner peace.
— *Richard Carlson*

It is always a good idea to be selfish with your temper.
— *Anonymous*

The life of patience and self-control helps to clear the mind, strengthen judgement and elevate one's character.
— *Benjamin Jowell*

Be strong enough to control your anger instead of letting it control you.
— *Anonymous*

"He who reins within himself and rules passions, desires, and fears is more than a king."

— John Milton

Our patience will achieve more than our force.
— *Edmund Burke*

A handful of patience is worth more than a bushel of brains.
— *Dutch Proverb*

Patience is genius.
— *Conte de Buffon*

Rome was not built in a day.
— *Proverb*

In any contest between power and patience, bet on patience.
— *W. B. Prescott*

If we want to exercise self-control, we must first learn how to demonstrate self-respect and practice self-talk.

Patience can help one to avoid problems and create possibilities.

Crises and conflict may reveal one's character while self-control strengthens it.

"Perseverance shows not only in the ability to persist but in the ability to start over."

— F. Scott Fitzgerald

When you come to the end
of your rope, tie and knot and hang on.
— *Franklin D. Roosevelt*

Perseverance is the result
of the will forcing itself
into the place of the intellect.
— *Arthur Schopenhauser*

Perseverance is another name for success.
— *Anonymous*

To succeed —
do the best you can,
all the time you can,
where you are,
and with what you have.
— *Oscar Arias*

PERSEVERANCE & DETERMINATION

Quotations

"Many of life's failures are people who did not realize how close they were to success when they gave up."

— Arabian Proverb

Character cannot be developed in ease and quiet. Only through the experience of trial and suffering can the soul be strengthened, ambition inspired and success achieved.
— *Helen Keller*

Perseverance is patience concentrated.
— *Thomas Carlyle*

I do the best I know how — the very best I can; and I mean to keep on doing so until the end.
— *Abraham Lincoln*

Perseverance is the crowning quality of great hearts.
— *James Russell Lovell*

"It's not whether you get knocked down. It's whether you get back up again."

— Ralph Waldo Emerson

The price of success is perseverance.
— *Anonymous*

The difference between the possible and the impossible lies in a person's determination.
— *Tommy Lasorda*

Keep trying. It's only from the valley that the mountain seems high.
— *Anonymous*

Never, never, never give up!
— *Winston Churchill*

Effort only reveals its reward after a person refuses to quit.
— *Napolean Hill*

"The journey of a thousand miles starts with a single step."

— Chinese Proverb

The harder you work the luckier you get.
— *Gary Player*

The difference between the ordinary and the extraordinary is that little extra effort called perseverance.
— *Chinese Proverb*

In the middle of difficulty lies opportunity.
— *Albert Einstein*

Failure usually follows the path of least persistence.
— *Anonymous*

Perseverance is the greatest of all teachers.
— *Arabian Proverb*

"You are never a loser until you quit trying."

— Mike Ditka

A jug fills drop by drop.
— *Buddha*

Perseverance is not a long race;
it is many short races one after another.
— *Walter Elliott*

You win some, you lose some,
and some get rained out,
but you gotta suit up for them all.
— *J. Askenberg*

The difference between perseverance
and obstinacy is that one often comes
from a strong will, and the other
from a strong won't.
— *Henry Ward Beecher*

"Character consists of what you do on the third and fourth tries."

— John Albert Michener

Knowing that troubles produce perseverance; and perseverance character; and character hope.
— *The Apostle Paul*

The world was built to develop character, and we must learn that setbacks and griefs which we endure help us in our marching onward.
— *Henry Ford*

Determination is the wake-up call to the human will.
— *Anthony Robbins*

They say love will find a way. I know determination will.
— *Ronnie Milsap*

When you think your
will is gone, remember
the importance of keepin' on.

Perseverance is the benchmark
for one's strength of character.

Life's challenges present us
with three basic choices:
give in; give up; or go on.

Quotations
from the Author

"Respect is the moral conscience of the great."

— Anonymous

Respect is the thread that weaves throughout all human encounters.
— *Anonymous*

Treat men greatly and they
will show themselves to be great.
— *Anonymous*

Respect yourself, if you would
have others respect you.
— *Baltassi Gracian*

Respect for oneself and others is the
precondition of any ethical action.
— *Oscar Arias*

Do right. Do the best you can. Treat others
the way you would want to be treated.
— *Lou Holtz*

"Respect and honor are the best memorial for a mighty man."

— Beowulf

Respect is the ultimate compliment.
— *Anonymous*

Respect is purchased by the deeds we do.
— *Christopher Marlowe*

I would rather man should ask why no statue has been erected in my honor, than why one has.
— *Marcus Cato*

It is better to be hated for what you are than to be loved for what you are not.
— *André Gide*

Respect does not come from possessing honors but in deserving them.
—*Aristotle*

"Be respectful yourself, if you wish to associate with respectful people."

— Welsh Proverb

To be capable of respect is almost
as rare as to be worthy of it.
— *John Joubert*

Character is the formation stone
upon which one must build to earn respect.
— *R.C. Samsel*

Self-respect is like weaving a coat
of armor that no one can cut through.
— *Henry Wadsworth Longfellow*

If you expect respect,
be the first to show it.
— *Anonymous*

When we do good things, our self-respect grows.
— *Heschel*

"Respect is learned, earned and returned."

— Anonymous

Every action in the company of others ought to be done with some sign of respect to those present.
— *George Washington*

Self-respect is the fruit of discipline; the sense of dignity grows with the ability to say no to oneself.
— *Abraham Hesched*

Respect is love in plain clothes.
— *Frankie Byrne*

I must respect the opinions of others even if I disagree with them.
— *Herbert Henry Lehman*

Respect commands itself and it can neither be given nor withheld when it is due.
— *Eldridge Cleaver*

"The soul that is within me no man can degrade."

— Frederick Douglas

This above all;
to thine own self be true.
— *William Shakespeare*

My honor is my loyalty.
— *Heinrich Himmler*

Respect — not tolerance — must be
our goal if we would diminish
prejudice in our time.
— *Selma G. Hirsch*

Where talent is a dwarf,
self-esteem is a giant.
— *J. Petit-Senn*

Our own heart, and not
other men's opinion,
forms our true honor.
— *Samuel Taylor Coleridge*

Respect is the reward
for what you give to others.

You know what's right.
Respect yourself and others,
and do what's right.

Respect involves an appraisal
of ourselves first, and then others.

"Every right has its responsibilities."

— Lewis Schwellenbach

A man's work is a great portrait of himself.
— *Anonymous*

There are three responsibilities — responsibility for self and social responsibility toward others and the community.
— *Amatai Etzioni*

Working hard may not make you rich, but it will make you successful.
— *Margaret Thatcher*

Never put off 'til tomorrow what you can do today ... never trouble another for what you can do yourself.
— *Thomas Jefferson*

"I hope to accomplish a great and noble task, but it is my chief duty to accomplish small tasks that are great and noble."

— Helen Keller

Do everything you ought to do.
— *Anonymous*

It is easy to dodge our responsibilities, but we cannot dodge the consequences of dodging our responsibility.
— *Anonymous*

Responsibility is the great developer.
— *Louis Brandeis*

You cannot escape the responsibilities of tomorrow by evading them today.
— *Anonymous*

Those who shrink from responsibility keep on shrinking in other ways too.
— *Anonymous*

"Our responsibility: every opportunity an obligation; every possession a duty."

— John D. Rockefeller

Responsibility is the thing people dread most of all; yet, it is the one thing that develops us.
— *Mark Twain*

You can never do more than your duty;
you should never do less.
— *Robert E. Lee*

Responsibility belongs to the person, regardless of age.
— *Robert Martin*

I am what I am today because
of the choices I made yesterday.
— *Anonymous*

Responsibility is the price of greatness.
— *Winston Churchill*

"**Hold yourself responsible to a higher standard than anyone expects of you.**"

— Henry Ward Beecher

The price of greatness is responsibility.
— *Winston Churchill*

Few things help an individual more than to place responsibility upon him, and to let him know that you trust him.
— *Booker T. Washington*

The ability to accept responsibility is the measure of the man.
— *Roy Williams*

What is your duty? Whatever the day calls for?
— *Johann Goethe*

We need to restore the full meaning of that old word, duty. It is the other side of rights.
— *Pearl Buck*

"Responsibility walks hand in hand with capacity and power."

— Josiah Gilbert Holland

Whatever happens, take responsibility.
— *Anthony Robbins*

When we have begun
to take charge of our lives,
to own ourselves, there is no longer
any need to ask permission of someone.
— *George O'Neil*

If you load responsibility
on a man unworthy of it
he will always betray himself.
— *August Heckscher*

We have a Bill of Rights. What we need
is a Bill of Responsibilities.
— *Bill Maher*

You either choose to do what's right or you choose to do what's wrong. The consequences of your choice affects you and others.

Acceptance of responsibility will show a person to be far stronger than was imagined.

When you accept responsibility, you personally grow.

"ALONE WE CAN DO SO LITTLE; TOGETHER WE CAN DO SO MUCH."

— HELEN KELLER

Teamwork is coming together
to accomplish a common goal.
— *Anonymous*

We must all hang together, or
most assuredly we will all hang separately.
— *Benjamin Franklin*

If he works for you, you work for him.
— *Anonymous*

The nice thing about teamwork
is that you always have
others on your side.
— *Margaret Carty*

The two things that bring
people together are fear and interest.
— *Napoleon I*

"We must learn to live together as brothers or perish together as foes."

— Dr. Martin Luther King, Jr.

All for one and one for all.
— *Alexander Dumas*

You cannot help someone without helping yourself.
— *Anonymous*

A house divided against itself cannot stand.
— *Abraham Lincoln*

United we stand, divided we fall.
— *Aesop*

TEAM: Together Everyone Achieves More.
— *Anonymous*

"It is not in numbers but in unity that our great strength lies."

— Thomas Paine

A single twig may break,
but a bundle of twigs is strong.
— *Tecumseh*

A job is easier when
a lot of people share it.
— *Homer*

The law of life should not be competition,
but cooperation, the good of each
contributing to the good of all.
— *Jawahardal Nehrue*

There can be no they,
only we.
— *Anonymous*

Many hands make light work.
— *John Heywood*

"The moment we break faith with one another, the sea engulfs us and the light goes out."

— James Baldwin

No problem is insurmountable. With a little courage, teamwork and determination, a person can overcome anything.
— *B. Dodge*

Coming together is a beginning, staying together is progress.
— *Henry Ford*

People have been known to achieve more as a result of working with others than against them.
— *Dr. Allan Fromme*

"The achievements of an organization are the results of the combined effort of each individual."

— Vince Lombardi

The way a team plays as a whole determines its success. You may have the greatest bunch of individual stars in the world, but if they don't play together, the club won't be worth a dime.
— *Babe Ruth*

Individuals play the game, but teams win championships.
— *Anonymous*

When he took time
to help the man up the mountain,
lo, he scaled it himself.
— *Anonymous*

Quotations

Teamwork begins
with saying, "We will".

Teamwork is coming together,
staying together and doing together.

Teamwork is the ability
to work together and
share common sacrifices.

"Trust is the highest form of human motivation."

— Stephen Covey

Trust is a passionate intuition.
— *Anonymous*

Trust is an assent of the mind
and a consent of the heart.
— *E.T. Hiscox*

Trust helps the soul ride at anchor.
— *John Billings*

Trust underlies the
foundation of civilization.
— *W. Bourke Cockran*

Trust is the feeling that makes
one man believe in another.
— *Henry Louis Menchen*

TRUST

Quotations

"Trust is what every great pioneering people have."

— Ben Yehuda

Trust, but verify.
— *Russian Proverb*

Trust, like the soul, never returns once it is gone.
— *Publibius*

Trust is the only bond of friendship.
— *Syrus*

You must first trust in yourself before you can trust others.
— *Anonymous*

No one can trust for us.
— *Sue Halpern*

"Trust everyone until you have reason not to."

— Anonymous

Trust people, and they
will be true to you.
— *Ralph Waldo Emerson*

Trust one who
has gone through it.
— *Virgil*

It is impossible to go
through life without trust;
that is to be imprisoned
in the worst cell of all — oneself.
— *Graham Henry Greene*

You may be deceived if
you trust too much, but you will live
in torment if you don't trust enough.
— *Frank Crane*

"The man who trusts men will make fewer mistakes than he who distrusts them."

— Camillo Benso Conte Di Cavour

Woe to the man whose heart
has not learned while young
to hope, to love — and
to put its trust in life.
— *Joseph Conrad*

Who would not rather trust
and be deceived?
— *Eliza Cook*

She knew how to trust people ...
a rare quality, revealing a character
far above average.
— *Cardinal Jean Francois de Retz*

If you can't trust people,
who can you trust?
— *Hohn Widdiconbe*

"Trust thyself: every heart vibrates to that iron string."

— Ralph Waldo Emerson

Trust dies but mistrust blossoms.
— *Sophocles*

It is an equal failing to trust everybody, and to trust nobody.
— *18th Century English Proverb*

Love all, trust a few,
Do wrong to none.
— *William Shakespeare*

The best proof of love is trust.
— *Joyce Brothers*

Mistrust makes life difficult.
Trust makes it risky.
— *Mason Cooley*

Trust builds relationships.
Relationships build people.

Trust is the healing ointment
of the soul.

If you are unwilling
to trust, prepare to be lonely.

Activities

Activity 1: The Ugly Duckling

Read the story *The Ugly Duckling* (written by Hans Christian Andersen) and discuss how the duckling felt when others teased or ignored him. Why did the duck want to run away?

Ask students to generate a list of ways we can be a friend to another person, show we care, and show respect. Write these ideas on the board.

Emphasize how people can look different on the outside, but everyone has feelings and we all need the caring and support of others to feel included.

Activity 2: Ways to Show Kindness

Discuss caring, compassion and kindness with the class. Ask students to contribute ways we can show kindness to each other (sharing, not interrupting, making friends, not fighting, etc.). Write these ideas on the board.

Activity 3: I Think You Are Great Because...

Prior to the activity, make a poster using construction paper for each student with his or her name, picture and the words "I think you are great because…"

As a class, brainstorm positive words that we can use to describe people. You may wish to record some of these ideas on the board for reference.

Place the posters around the room and assign a student to each poster (not their own). Tell the children to write a positive statement about the child on the poster. Have the students rotate around the room to make sure they get to sign every poster.

Activity 1: Character Compliment Magnets

Make a list of all students in the class. Have each student write compliments about the other students and turn them in.

Edit and type the compliments on labels. Give students their "labels of compliments." Ask a local business to donate magnets and have the students select a compliment to place on their magnet.

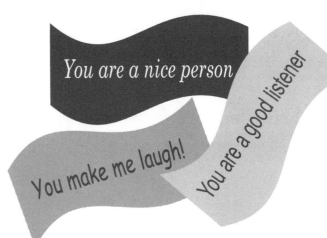

You are a nice person

You make me laugh!

You are a good listener

Activity 2: Act of Kindness Journal

Ask that each student create a "Kindness Journal" out of paper and decorate the cover. Each time they see or hear another student display or say an act of kindness, they should write it in their journal and date it.

Once a week, students can share from their kindness journals with the class.

Activity 3: The Caring Tree

Read Shel Silverstein's book, *The Giving Tree*, to students. Discuss how caring is used in the story.

Have each student write at least one "caring comment" about another classmate on a leaf pattern previously cut out. Have a large tree on the bulletin board, and allow students to place their leaves on the tree.

Activity 1: Community Service for Character

As a class, discuss a community project that the class could do to demonstrate caring, kindness, initiative and perseverance. Spend time planning the activity and implementing the activity.

Afterwards, have students discuss or write about their experience.

Activity 2: Character Songs

Have students break into small groups and write an original song or rap about kindness. Allow the groups to use music if they would like.

Record the songs using a cassette recorder if possible, and play for the class.

Activity 3: Kindness Role Play

In small groups, ask students to develop a two- or three-minute skit that shows the benefits of caring, compassion and kindness in our daily lives.

Have each group present its skit to the class.

Activity 1: The Pledge of Allegiance

As a class, memorize the Pledge of Allegiance (if not already in place in the classroom). Discuss that the flag is our national symbol, and explain what the Stars and Stripes stand for. In what other ways do we show patriotism? At parades? July 4th? Etc.?

Activity 2: Color the Flag

Pass out an outline of the American Flag to each student. Allow them to create their version of the American Flag using pencils, crayons, etc. Display the creations in the classroom.

Activity 3: Take Pride in America

Discuss how we can take pride in the country, state, city and community where we live. Some examples may include staying out of trouble, not littering, recycling, volunteering, paying taxes, etc. Ask the students to share their ideas about how they can show good citizenship. Write the ideas on the board.

Activity 1: Dear America

Ask each student to write a poem entitled "Dear America." Ask them to concentrate on what America means to them.

Those who wish may share their poems with the class.

Activity 2: What is a Good Citizen?

Have a group discussion concerning what it takes to be a good citizen. Ask students what lifeskills are important. Honesty? Integrity? Kindness? Etc.?

Activity 3: Independence Day

Spend one class studying about the 4th of July, Independence Day. Break students into small groups and ask them to role-play a scene from this important day in history.

Activity 1: Flag Essay

Ask each student to research the American Flag and write a two-page essay. Each essay may contain answers to questions such as: What symbols are used in the flag (stars, stripes)? What do they represent? Who designed the flag? Ask students to share their essays with the class.

Have a group discussion concerning citizenship and patriotism. How is the flag used as a symbol of citizenship and patriotism in our country?

Activity 2: Dear America

Ask each student to write a poem entitled "Dear America." Ask them to concentrate on what America means to them.

Those who wish may share their poems with the class.

Activity 3: The Armed Forces

Separate students into four groups. As a homework assignment, ask students to research one branch of the armed forces. Ask each group to prepare a ten-minute oral presentation on their topic. They may include drawings, photographs or other visual aids in their presentation.

Activity 1: What Does Courage Look Like?

Give students pieces of paper and ask them to draw a picture of someone displaying courage. They may draw someone saying no to drugs, speaking in front of a class, etc. Display the artwork in the classroom when the project is completed.

Activity 2: Courage Role-Play

Separate students into small groups and have them role-play scenarios in which one person displays courage. After the skits, discuss ways that we can be courageous in our daily lives.

Activity 3: A Courageous Person

List some notable people on the board and discuss their displays of courage. Was Columbus courageous? Or Rosa Parks? How about George Washington?

What about present day people like firefighters and police officers? Are they courageous? Share more ideas of courageous people with the class.

Activity 1: Gone Fishin'

Give each student a ¼ size piece of paper. Have them fold it in half. On the upper half, have them write down something they are, or were, afraid of. On the lower half, have them write what they did or can do to help get over this fear.

Punch a hole through the top of both pieces of paper near the fold, then attach a paper clip. Have the students place the pieces of paper in a can.

Give students a "fishing pole" with a magnet attached to the end. Have them drop the end of the pole into the can and the magnet will attach itself to a paper clip.

The students "reel in" the clip of paper and read whatever is on the card. Make sure each student has a turn. Discuss the importance of courage.

Activity 2: Quote Discussion

Have a group discussion concerning the quote, "Stand up for what is right, even if you stand alone" (anonymous). What does this quote mean? Discuss the difficulties sometimes faced by being courageous in the face of peer pressure or other issues.

Activity 3: Courageous Essay

Ask students to write a short essay about someone they know who has done something courageous. Once the assignment is completed, ask for volunteers to read their essays to the class.

Activity 1: Courage Essay

Ask students to write a two-page essay concerning a time when they had to demonstrate exceptional courage. Ask them to discuss if choosing courage was a difficult decision. Some examples of experiences may be when a student stood up to peer pressure, had the courage to speak up against someone more popular or powerful, etc.

Activity 2: Quote Discussion

Have a group discussion concerning the quote, "The ultimate measure of a man is not where he stands in moments of comfort and convenience, but where he stands in times of challenge and controversy" (Martin Luther King, Jr.). What does this quote mean? Discuss the issues and difficulties sometimes faced by students under pressure, and the issues presented by facing these experiences with courage.

Activity 3: Courage Role Play

Separate students into small groups and ask them to develop a short skit concerning having courage in the face of pressure. Students should show one or more people in the skit displaying courage even when it may be difficult to do so (under peer pressure, standing up for an unpopular belief, taking up for a friend, etc.). Each group should present its skit to the class.

Activity 1: Say Please

Ask your students to call out courtesy statements we use every day including please, thank you, you are welcome, etc. Discuss when we use these statements, and how it makes us feel when we hear them/don't hear them.

Make a list of the courtesy statements on the board and put a check mark next to each statement each time it is used in class.

> Let's Be Courteous!
> ☑ Please
>
> ☑ Thank You
>
> ☑ You're Welcome
>
> ☑ Excuse Me

Activity 2: The Courtesy Award

Split your students into two small groups and have them each make a courtesy award. The award could be made out of construction paper and be decorated any way the group wishes.

Once the awards are complete, discuss as a class the traits associated with courtesy, politeness and manners. Keep the awards taped to the bulletin board at the front of the class. Once each day, decide as a class two individuals that deserve the awards for displaying courtesy, politeness and manners, and allow those students to wear the award for the rest of the day.

Activity 3: More Than Words

As a class, discuss that there is more to having courtesy, being polite and displaying good manners than the words we say. Have students discuss ways to display these positive character traits through body language (shaking hands, not rolling our eyes, not interrupting others when they speak, eating with utensils, using our napkin, etc.).

Have each student pick a new way they can display these positive character traits. Have each student commit to putting that new idea into practice for the week. At the end of the week, discuss the activity again. Did it feel good to be more courteous, polite and mannerly?

Activity 1: TV Courtesy

Ask students to watch their favorite TV show and write down the courtesy words they hear during the show (please, thank you, you are welcome, etc.). Was there a time you should have heard them, and didn't? Were the people or characters on the show displaying proper manners? Share the findings with the class.

Activity 2: Table Manners

As a class activity, design a large piece of construction paper or bulletin board to look like a place setting at a table. Have each student write down an example of proper table manners (napkin in lap, eating with utensils, chewing food well, not talking with your mouth full, wiping mouth with napkin, etc.) on a smaller piece of construction paper. Affix the examples to the larger board as you discuss the importance of proper table manners.

Activity 3: Class Discussion

Discuss the importance of being courteous, polite and mannerly in our daily lives. How do we feel when people don't treat us this way? Is it always important to be mindful of these lifeskills, or only with adults? How do you treat those who are mannerly to you?

Activity 1: Courtesy Charades

Write down examples of rudeness and discourtesy on sheets of paper. Have students volunteer to pick a sheet of paper out of a hat and act out that example in pairs (for example, interrupting one another, cutting in line, not saying please or thank you, etc.).

Have the other students guess what the discourteous example is, then discuss ways to show proper courtesy and manners in the same situations.

Activity 2: Cursing

Ask students to write a one-page essay concerning cursing (ask them to not include examples of curse words in their papers). How does it make them feel to hear these words spoken by others, in music and on television?

How does it make them feel when (if) they say them? Discuss the essays in class.

Activity 3: Class Courtesy Constitution

As a class, develop a "Class Courtesy Constitution" that can be posted on a wall or bulletin board. Ask students to brainstorm rules and regulations concerning courtesy, politeness and manners that all in the class will abide by.

Once the constitution is complete, post it in the classroom and give a copy to all students.

Activity 1: Telling the Truth Feels Good

Give students a sheet of paper and ask them to draw a self-portrait of what they look like when they tell the truth. On the other side of the sheet, ask them to draw a self-portrait of what they look like when they lie.

Allow students to take their papers home and share them with their parents.

Activity 2: Honest Abe

Share information on Abraham Lincoln with the class. Explain his nickname, "Honest Abe." Would that be a good reputation to have? Why is it important to tell the truth? Have students share their thoughts on lying.

Activity 3: Secret or Lie?

Hold a class discussion concerning the differences and similarities between secrets and lies. Are there times when you should keep a secret? Give examples of secrets that are appropriate (birthday gifts, surprise party) and in contrast, the inappropriate act of lying.

Activity 1: Honesty is the Best Policy

Ask students to write an essay concerning the statement "Honesty is the Best Policy." Is this always the case? Are there times when it is tempting to tell a "white lie?" How does our conscience feel when we lie? Ask those who are willing to share their essays with the class. Discuss.

Note: This activity may lead to discussions concerning "moral relativism" or "situational ethics". Instructors should try to encourage truth-telling in all situations and steer students away from justifying telling a lie in certain situations.

Activity 2: Truthfulness Contract

Ask students to write their own Truthfulness Contract. The contract is the student's promise to himself or herself to strive to always tell the truth to themselves and others. Once the students write the words, they may wish to decorate their contract on a sheet of construction paper. Each student should sign his or her contract. If the students wish, ask them to share their contracts with the class.

Activity 3: Role Play

Ask students to break into groups and create skits depicting students either telling the truth or lying in a pressure situation. After each skit, discuss the results. Why did the person lie or tell the truth? What does that say about the person's character?

Note: This activity may lead to discussions concerning "moral relativism" or "situational ethics". Instructors should try to encourage truth-telling in all situations and steer students away from justifying telling a lie in certain situations.

Activity 1: Honesty and Integrity

Hold a class discussion concerning honesty and integrity. What are definitions of each? How does being honest aide us in having integrity? On the board, write the following quote for students to reflect on: "Honesty is telling other people the truth; integrity is telling yourself the truth" (Spencer Johnson).

Activity 2: Honesty is the Best Policy

Ask students to write an essay concerning the statement "Honesty is the Best Policy." Is this always the case? Are there times when it is tempting to tell a "white lie?" How does our conscience feel when we lie? Ask those who are willing to share their essays with the class. Discuss.

Note: This activity may lead to discussions concerning "moral relativism" or "situational ethics". Instructors should try to encourage truth-telling in all situations and steer students away from justifying telling a lie in certain situations.

Activity 3: Role Play

Ask students to break into groups and create skits depicting students either telling the truth or lying in a pressure situation. After each skit, discuss the results. Why did the person lie or tell the truth? What does that say about the person's character?

Note: This activity may lead to discussions concerning "moral relativism" or "situational ethics". Instructors should try to encourage truth-telling in all situations and steer students away from justifying telling a lie in certain situations.

Activity 1: Playing Fair

On a sheet of paper, ask each student to draw a picture showing themselves playing fairly with other children.

Discuss being a good sport, not cheating, etc.

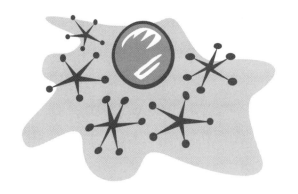

Activity 2: Proper Punishments

Have a class discussion concerning punishments. If a student breaks the rules at home, are they punished? What about at school? Is it fair to be punished for breaking a rule? Discuss the cause and effect between actions and consequences.

Activity 3: No Cheating

Discuss cheating in school with the class. Is cheating really a big deal? What does it say about your character? Is it fair for one person to study hard for good grades, and another to cheat and get the same grades? Does the student who cheats miss out on the learning opportunity studying brings?

Activity 1: You Be the Judge

Before the activity, write down on slips of paper different "crimes" like cheating on a test, disobeying a teacher, fighting and stealing. Have the students role play a scene where the "criminal" picks a crime from the hat and the "jury" decides his or her sentence. How harsh should the punishment for each crime be? Should the punishment for some be worse than others?

Discuss the justice and fairness of the punishments decided by the jury.

Activity 2: Fair Treatment

Have students discuss what it is like when you are not treated fairly. How does it feel? Discuss ways to correct unfair situations; what are the positive ways (following procedures, etc.) and negative ways (violence, etc.) to combat unfair treatment?

Activity 3: No Cheating

Discuss cheating in school with the class. Is cheating really a big deal? What does it say about your character? Is it fair for one person to study hard for good grades, and another to cheat and get the same grades? Does the student who cheats miss out on the learning opportunity studying brings?

Activity 1: In the News

Have students look for stories in the newspaper of people working to correct an unfair situation. Where did they turn for help? How did they make their issues known? Do you agree or disagree with their methods?

Activity 2: Justice Served

Bring in an article from the newspaper concerning a recent criminal and the punishment they received from the courts. Discuss the story with the students; was justice served? Discuss consequences of actions.

Activity 3: No Cheating

Discuss cheating in school with the class. Is cheating really a big deal? What does it say about your character? Is it fair for one person to study hard for good grades, and another to cheat and get the same grades? Does the student who cheats miss out on the learning opportunity studying brings?

Activity 1: A Picture of Patience

On a sheet of paper, ask students to draw a picture showing themselves in a situation where they have a hard time being patient. Some examples may be waiting to open a present, waiting for recess, wanting dessert before dinner, etc. Discuss the drawings and the rewards of being patient.

Activity 2: Discussing Self-Control

As a class, discuss the meaning of self-control. When do the students find it hard to control themselves? List these on the board. Examples may be talking out of turn in class, disobeying school rules, fighting, losing their temper, eating too much, etc. What are some ways we can show self-control? List these on the board as well.

Activity 3: The Windowsill Garden

As a class, allow students to plant seeds in pots for a windowsill garden. Discuss how it will take patience to wait until they grow big and strong. Map out a plan (watering schedule, etc.) for the class so each student can help achieve the goal.

As the plants begin to grow, revisit the subject of patience and discuss how we must sometimes wait patiently in order to reap the rewards of our efforts.

Activity 1: Character Mobile

For one week, have students look through magazines to find photos that emphasize patience and self-control (or the lack of them). Ask them to bring the pictures to class, or look through the magazines as a group.

The cut pictures should be glued to different sizes of poster board. Each student then can make his or her "character mobile." Be sure to affix a strip of poster board to the mobile that states the character trait.

Activity 2: Losing Control

As a class, discuss ways people lose self-control in their lives. Examples may include alcohol and drug addiction, anorexia and bulimia, working too much, excessive shopping, etc. Discuss the negative effects of losing self-control and the perseverance it takes to regain control in our lives.

Activity 3: Patience Essay

Ask the students to write a one-page essay on a personal experience when they lost their patience with another person (examples could be with another student, a younger sibling, etc.). Ask them to discuss how they felt after losing their temper, and what they did (if anything) to correct the situation. Students may include suggestions of ways to have more patience with others.

Activity 1: Losing Control to Drugs

Ask the students to write a two-page essay on drug addiction and the loss of control those addicted to drugs experience in their lives. Make sure the students research the topic and include positive steps those addicted can take to reverse their situation.

Activity 2: Patience Role Play

Ask students to develop skits in which one or more students lose their patience with someone else. After the skit, ask the person(s) who was not patient how he or she feels, then ask the person who was treated unfairly in the skit. Brainstorm ideas in which the persons could have maintained self-control in the situation. Ideas may include walking away from the situation, counting to ten, taking a deep breath, trying to put yourself in the other person's shoes, etc.

Activity 3: Patience Poem

Ask students to write a short poem about patience. For extra credit, hold a contest and allow the students to vote for the best poem.

Activity 1: The Little Engine That Could

Read the book *The Little Engine That Could* (written by Watty Piper) to the class. Discuss the lifeskills the little engine needed to get up the hill. Did his perseverance pay off?

Activity 2: Discussing Determination

Ask students to think of how it feels when they really want something badly for themselves or another person (like winning a sports event, buying something at the store, saving up allowance to buy a present for Mom or Dad, etc.). What would they do to achieve that goal? Discuss how perseverance and determination pay off for those who struggle to meet their goals.

Activity 3: Hands of Perseverance

Obtain a copy of the sign language alphabet from the library or the Internet. Make copies and use as a handout for students.

Using the handout, teach students to spell out the words perseverance and determination as you discuss their meanings. Allow older students to take turns spelling out words that represent perseverance and determination. Some examples of words include focused; fixed; determined; firm; settled; resolved; sure; positive; and steadfast.

Activity 1: Perseverance is ...

Ask students to finish the sentence "Perseverance is ..." Have them write down as many examples as possible to complete this sentence. Share with the class.

Activity 2: Community Service for Character

As a class, discuss a community project that the class could do to demonstrate caring, kindness, initiative and perseverance. Spend a week planning the activity and two to five days implementing the activity. Have students discuss or write about their experience.

Activity 3: Procrastination

As a class, discuss what procrastination is and why it can be damaging to us. Have students list things that are easy to put off until later (chores, homework, studying for a test, etc.). As a class, discuss ways to combat procrastination.

Activity 1: Community Service for Character

As a class, discuss a community project that the class could do to demonstrate caring, kindness, initiative and perseverance. Spend a week planning the activity and two to five days implementing the activity.

Have students discuss or write about their experience.

Activity 2: Goal Setting

Ask the class to write individual essays concerning a goal they have set for themselves after graduation. Will they go to college? Get a job? Get married? Ask them to include their thoughts on why goal setting is important, and how perseverance and determination are important in reaching those goals.

Activity 3: Short Essay

Ask each student to research a person in history that showed tremendous perseverance and determination. Students should gain information on their subject and write a short essay on their struggle to achieve. Ask students to share their findings with the class.

Activity 1: Respecting Others

Discuss the word respect. How can we show respect to others? Ask the class for suggestions and write them on the board. Some ideas may be being friendly, playing fair, not hitting, saying please and thank you, smiling, not interrupting, etc.

Activity 2: Drawing Activity

Give students a sheet of paper and ask them to draw a scene showing themselves respecting another person. Some ideas may be interacting with a parent or grandparent, playing on the playground with friends, sharing, etc. Display the artwork in class after each student presents his or her scene to the other students.

Activity 3: Respect Collage

Bring magazines into the classroom and ask students to clip pictures that show people respecting themselves and one another. Ideas may include someone getting enough sleep, exercising, shaking hands with another person, playing fair, etc. Create a collage to hang in the classroom.

Activity 1: Role Models

Ask students to list three individuals in their lives (parents, relatives, teachers, friends, neighbors, etc.) who are examples of positive character role models. Discuss the list. Give students three index cards each and ask them to complete the sentence, "You, _____ , are a positive role model to me because you demonstrate the character trait(s) of _____." Ask students to share their responses with the class.

Activity 2: Respecting Ourselves

Cover a large bulletin board with construction paper. Draw a large puzzle piece on the board. Have enough pieces for each student to have a piece of the puzzle.

Have students glue a small picture of themselves on the puzzle pieces, then write a way they can respect themselves on them. Glue the pieces to the bulletin board.

Activity 3: Character "Ed"

On a piece of paper, trace or draw the outline of a young boy. Title him Character "Ed."

On one side of the boy, write "I will show respect for myself..." On the other side, write, "I will show respect for others..."

Copy the sheet and pass it out to students. Have them fill in each side with ways they can respect themselves and other people.

Activity 1: Music Messages

Ask students to bring songs to school that focus on respect. You may choose to use the songs listed on pages 151-152 of this book. (Make sure all songs played are appropriate before playing in front of the class). Play the songs for the class; discuss their messages as a group.

Activity 2: Showing Proper Respect

Ask students to research different signs of respect in various cultures. Some examples may be shaking hands, bowing, etc. Allow each student to present a short oral presentation to the class about what he or she found.

Activity 3: Respect Letter

Ask students to each pick one person they highly respect and write a letter to him or her. The person can be a family member, friend, instructor, neighbor or celebrity.

The students should include why they respect the person and how it makes them feel. Ask students to share with the class. (Letters can be given to the person if the students wish).

Activity 1: Taking Responsibility

Discuss the word responsibility and what it means. Ask students to share ways they can be responsible and help out at home. Have each student commit to one task they can be responsible for at home. Ask them to commit to their task for at least one week. Discuss at the end of the week how it feels to take responsibility for something.

Activity 2: Owning a Pet

Owning a pet can be fun, but it also takes responsibility to care for the animal. If your school allows, adopt a class pet (like a goldfish) and charge the students with the responsibility of taking care of it. Allow the students to take turns feeding, changing water, etc., with the teacher's help.

If your school does not allow pets, hold a discussion about caring for a pet. Ask those students with pets at home to discuss the responsibilities that come with pet ownership. Discuss the rewards that come with the responsibility, too.

Activity 3: I'm Responsible!

Give students sheets of paper and ask them to draw pictures describing their responsibilities at school. Their pictures may include depictions of arriving to school on time, completing homework, staying awake, trying their best, playing fair, paying attention in class, etc.

Have each student copy the words "I'm Responsible!" onto the top of their paper before turning in. Display the artwork on the walls of the classroom.

Activity 1: The Rewards of Responsibility

As a homework assignment, ask each student to interview a parent or close relative about a responsibility they have and the rewards that come from it. An example may be to interview a parent about his or her job and the rewards (money, vacation time and satisfaction for a job well done) received in return.

Ask each student to submit a short essay about the interview and what they learned. Pick several to read aloud to the class.

Activity 2: Responsible Role Play

Separate students into small groups and ask them to develop a short skit about responsibility. The students may choose to show a student taking responsibility for something, or being irresponsible. Allow each group to present to the class.

After all groups have completed the skits, discuss how being responsible helps build character.

Activity 3: Taking Responsibility

Discuss the word responsibility and what it means. Ask students to share ways they can be responsible and help out at home. Have students commit to one task they can be responsible for at home. Ask them to commit to their task for at least one week. Discuss at the end of the week how it feels to take responsibility for something.

Activity 1: Class Discussion

Discuss as a class the meaning of responsibility. How do you feel about accepting responsibility? How do you feel about people who will not accept responsibility for their own actions? Should you have to take responsibilities for your achievements and your mistakes? Break into small groups for further discussion.

Activity 2: Responsible Role Play

Separate students into small groups and ask them to develop a short skit about responsibility. The students may choose to show a student taking responsibility for something, or being irresponsible. Allow each group to present to the class.

After all groups have completed the skits, discuss how being responsible helps build character.

Activity 3: The Rewards of Responsibility

As a homework assignment, ask students to interview a parent or close relative about a responsibility they have and the rewards that come from it. Examples may be to interview a parent about his or her job and the rewards (money, vacation time and satisfaction for a job well done) that are received in return.

Ask students to submit a short essay about the interview and what they learned. Pick several to read aloud to the class.

Activity 1: Team Drawing

Ask students to draw a team on a sheet of paper. This team can be a sports team, work team, group of friends, etc. — anything the student wishes to create.

Ask students to present their drawings to the class and explain why teamwork is important to the group.

Activity 2: Three-Legged Race

On a nice day outside, take the students to an open area and separate them into pairs. Tie each pair of students' inside legs together with a bandanna or soft strip of cloth. (Be careful not to pair the most athletic kids together.)

Conduct a short race to a finish line. After the race, discuss the experience as a group. Was it difficult to work together on "three legs"? Who won? Did teamwork help them win?

Activity 3: Teamwork Mobile

Use construction paper to make a teamwork mobile, allowing each student to write his or her name on a cutout of a person. Allow each student to decorate the cutout using crayons, etc. String all of the people cutouts onto the mobile under the headline "We Make a Great Team!" Display the mobile in the classroom.

Activity 1: Link to Think

Have students write down problems they are having with classes, other students, homework, etc. They may do this anonymously. Provide strips of paper for the students to write on. Collect the strips when finished (you may choose to do this several times throughout the year).

Several times a week, read one or two of the problems to the class. Have the students work together to find solutions to the problems. If the students are successful at solving the problem, create a link out of the strip of paper and affix it to the bulletin board. Do this each time a problem is solved. By the end of the year, the linked chain will be quite long and will be a visual reminder of the benefits of teamwork and cooperation.

Activity 2: Three-Legged Race

On a nice day outside, take the students to an open area and separate them into pairs. Tie each pair of students' inside legs together with a bandanna or soft strip of cloth. (Be careful not to pair the most athletic kids together.)

Conduct a short race to a finish line. After the race, discuss the experience as a group. Was it difficult to work together on "three legs"? Who won? Did teamwork help them win?

Activity 3: Teamwork Poem

Ask each student to write a poem or song about teamwork. The students may include their thoughts on being part of a team, the value of cooperation, etc. Ask that all students submit their poems/songs without their names on their papers. From all poems and songs entered, as a class, vote on one poem/song that will be the official class motto on teamwork. If applicable, use school production equipment to produce a song or a short video.

Activity 1: Hand Twister

Have the students form a circle and grasp hands with others in the circle, but not those standing next to them. Without letting go, have the students twist and turn to untangle themselves until they form another circle.

Afterwards, discuss the teamwork and cooperation that went into the group succeeding (or failing) at the task.

Activity 2: Link to Think

Have students write down problems they are having with classes, other students, homework, etc. on strips of paper. They may do this anonymously. Collect the strips when finished (you may choose to do this several times throughout the year).

Several times a week, read one or two of the problems to the class. Have the students work together to find solutions to the problems. If the students are successful at solving the problem, create a link out of the strip of paper and affix it to the bulletin board. Do this each time a problem is solved. By the end of the year, the linked chain will be quite long and will be a visual reminder of the benefits of teamwork and cooperation.

Activity 3: Blindfolded Relay

Separate students into small groups. Pick one navigator for each group. Outside or in a clear area, create a predetermined obstacle course. You may use barrels, trashcans, etc. as obstacles. Make sure your course will allow participants to go through things, under things, around things, etc.

Blindfold all students except for the navigator in each group. The blindfolded groups start at the beginning of the course and must be "talked through" the obstacles by their navigators. The navigators should stand at the end of the course and can only help their teams by talking them through the obstacles. The first group to reach the finish line wins.

After the exercise, discuss how teamwork and cooperation influenced the activity. Was cooperation important between the navigator and group? Among the members of the group?

Activity 1: Who Can You Trust?

Ask students to share some of the people in their lives that they can trust. List these people on the board. The list may include parents, siblings, other relatives, friends, religious leaders, doctors, etc. Is there anyone the students do not trust? Reemphasize that trust must be earned. You may wish to include a short discussion on strangers, and that we should not trust them, go with them, etc.

Activity 2: Trust is Earned

Hold a class discussion concerning what trust is, and that is must be earned. How do we earn another person's trust? Discuss the importance of being honest, reliable and dependable in gaining trust.

Activity 3: Trust Walk

In the classroom, ask the students to form a single file line. Ask them to place a hand on the shoulder of the person in front of them and close their eyes. With the teacher as the line leader, take the students on a short "trust walk" around the classroom. Discuss the experience afterwards; was it scary to trust the person in front of you?

Activity 1: Ways I Am Trustworthy

Give each student a sheet of paper with the words "I Demonstrate I Am Trustworthy By…" on it. Ask students to list five ways they demonstrate trustworthiness on a daily basis, including telling the truth, being dependable, taking responsibility for their own actions, etc. Share the lists as a group.

Activity 2: Earning Trust

Ask each student to write a one-page essay on the importance of earning trust from others. What other life skills must be demonstrated to earn trust? What life skill traits do we look for in a trustworthy person?

Activity 3: Trust Walk

Separate students into pairs. Blindfold one student in each pair, and have the other student lead them outside, over and around objects, kindly telling them where to go and things to watch out for, since they cannot see. After five minutes, reverse the roles.

Return to the classroom and have the students discuss what lifeskills they experienced (trust is the main theme, but students experience others during the event). Discuss that trust is the beginning of forming a good relationship.

Activity 1: Trust Walk

Separate students into pairs. Blindfold one student in each pair, and have the other student lead them outside, over and around objects, kindly telling them where to go and things to watch out for, since they cannot see. After five minutes, reverse the roles.

Return to the classroom and have the students discuss what lifeskills they experienced (trust is the main theme, but students experience others during the event). Discuss that trust is the beginning of forming a good relationship.

Activity 2: Defining Truth

Before the activity, write words not often used on strips of paper with the definition of the word below. Place the strips of paper in a hat.

As a class, allow students to draw words from the hat, then explain the word and definition to the class. The student has the choice of repeating the correct definition or making one up. The class will then vote on whether the student gave the correct definition of the word.

After the game is over, discuss lying and how it feels to be lied to. As in this case, the lie wasn't damaging, or was it? Is it ever appropriate to lie? How does being lied to affect your trust in the person lying?

Activity 3: Trust Essay

Ask students to write an essay concerning a time in their lives when they had to place trust in another person. Afterwards, ask if any student would like to share his or her essay with the class.

Bulletin Board Ideas

Caring Makes the World Go Round

Decorate a bulletin board with an Earth symbol and children holding hands around it. Use the headline "Caring *Makes the World Go Around!" to emphasize these lifeskills.*

Kindness is Shining in Our Classroom!

Decorate a bulletin board using a lighthouse theme. Use the headline "Kindness is Shining in Our Classroom!" From the light in the lighthouse, use strips of paper to denote the light shining out into the darkness. On each strip, write *an example of how we can show kindness to others, such as helping our parents, sharing, being friendly to others, not teasing our siblings, showing compassion to those less fortunate and being kind to animals.*

We're Good Citizens

Decorate a bulletin board using a picture of a young person being a good citizen by following a posted rule: Dogs must be on a leash. Use the words "Good Citizens are Cool and Follow the Rules!"

Flags of Patriotism

Ask students to make individual flags depicting what it means to them to be an American. They can use various colors, pictures from home, text or other designs to create their flag. Arrange the completed flags on a bulletin board under the title "We are Proud to be Americans!"

It Takes Courage

Decorate a bulletin board with a large star, with smaller shooting stars around the larger one. In the middle of the large star, use the headline "It Takes Courage to Have Great Character!" to emphasize this lifeskill. In the smaller stars, you may choose to write some examples of courage, including standing up for your beliefs, telling the truth, respecting others, etc.

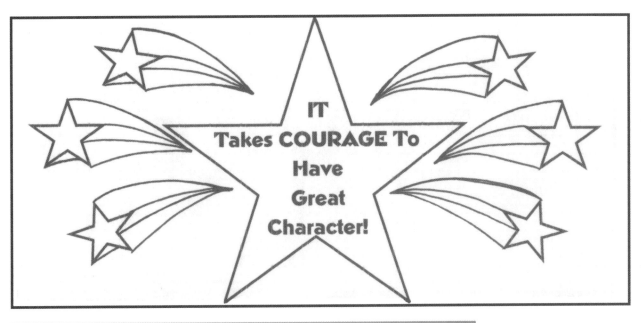

Courage is Contagious: Catch it Today!

Decorate a bulletin board with the images of several groups of children in a specific encounter like being offered cigarettes, drugs, alcohol, etc. Use the headline "Courage is Contagious: Catch it Today!"

Bee Kind and Courteous

Decorate a bulletin board with a stop sign symbol with "Bad Manners" written underneath it. Create a bumble bee and add the words "Bee Kind" and "Bee Courteous" to the board.

The Words of Kindness

Decorate a bulletin board with a child's image and balloon text symbols coming from his or her mouth. In the balloons, add the words of kindness (please, thank you, you are welcome, etc.)

The Path to Good Character

Decorate a bulletin board with different maps, or draw your own. Use the headline "Honesty is the Path to Good Character!" You may choose to label the streets with traits like truthfulness, dependability, etc.

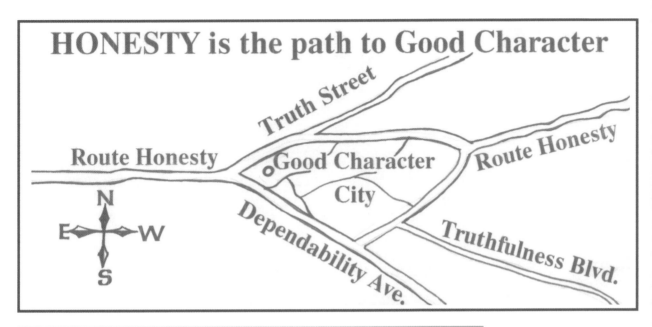

Lighten Your Heart

Decorate a bulletin board with a large lightbulb and small hearts. Use the headline "Truthfulness Lightens Your Heart!"

Be a Winner...Play Fair!

Decorate a bulletin board with pictures of various people playing different types of sports. Use large cutouts of softballs, bats, soccer balls, basketballs, etc., to emphasize the sports theme. Use the headline "Be a Winner … Play Fair!" to emphasize fair competition.

Fairness Helps You Fly High

Decorate a bulletin board with a large airplane, or with several birds. Use the headline "Fairness Helps You Fly High!"

Practice Patience

Decorate a bulletin board with a snow scene including a sun and a melting *snowman. Use the headline "Don't Lose Your Cool … Practice Patience!"*

Our Class Practices Self-Control!

Decorate a bulletin board with various symbols and shapes like circles, stars, squares, triangles, etc. Use the words "Our Class Practices Self-Control!" in the middle of the board. In each shape, write *ways to show self control and patience, including waiting our turn, not interrupting, raising our hand in class, controlling our anger, no violence, saying no to drugs, etc.*

Perseverance Pays Off!

Decorate a bulletin board with a large hot air balloon and the words "Perseverance Pays Off!" In clouds around the hot air balloon, write examples of perseverance and determination, including doing your personal best, taking pride in accomplishment, finishing what you start, being motivated, etc.

Perseverance Shines Through

Decorate a bulletin board with a large gold star. Use the words "Perseverance Shines Through" as a headline. In smaller stars around the larger one, write ways to show perseverance and determination like being a goal setter, being confident, being a risk taker, not quitting, being prepared, being on time, etc.

Respect: Learn it, Know it, Show it!

Decorate a bulletin board using the theme "Respect: Learn it, Know it, Show it!" Use any type of design you wish to convey different ways to show respect, such as being polite, respecting your elders, not interrupting, taking care of your and other's belongings, etc.

Respect Yourself!

Decorate a bulletin board using the words "Respect Yourself" and a large image of a child. Decorate the image with smaller designs including ways to respect oneself, including getting enough sleep, saying no to drugs, exercising and eating healthy.

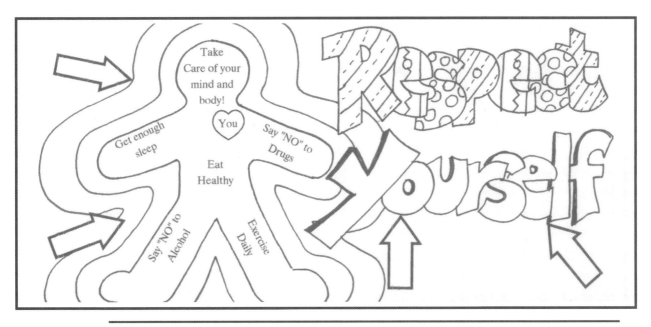

Bulletin Board Ideas

You are Responsible

Decorate a bulletin board with a responsibility theme by using the sentence "You are Responsible for Your Own Actions!" Use different colors and fonts to make the bulletin board attractive. You can also make some words (you, responsible) larger for added emphasis.

Key to Good Character

Decorate a bulletin board with a large key and the words "Responsibility is the Key to Good Character!"

We Can Do it Together!

Decorate a bulletin board with a teamwork theme by placing cutouts of children holding hands on the board.

Under the children, use the words "We Can Do it — Together!"

Class Cooperation

Decorate a bulletin board with a cooperation theme with the headline "Class Cooperation Helps Us Achieve Our Best!" List your class philosophy,

including putdowns are prohibited; respect and trust each other; insist upon your personal best; discuss and listen actively; and expect and give truth and honesty.

Do Unto Others

Decorate a bulletin board showing two children shaking hands. Use the headline "Tell the Truth." Underneath the picture, use the subhead "Remember the Golden Rule … Do Unto Others As You Would Have Them Do Unto You!"

Place Your Trust in Others

Decorate a bulletin board with the image of a basket. Fill the basket with cutouts of apples. Depict a few more apples going into the basket with the words, "Place Your Trust in Others!"

Song Titles

With Moral and Inspirational Messages

The following songs have been listed for the positive moral and inspirational messages they contain. Songs on records, cassette tapes or CD's are great ways to teach character messages to students.

You may wish to include one or more of these songs in a character education activity. Play a song and have students write down the messages and character words/themes they hear; then, break into small groups to discuss. Have students share the messages they heard with the class, and suggest other songs with moral messages.

40 Songs with Moral and Inspirational Messages

Song Title	Artist	Album/CD
American Trilogy	Elvis Presley	This is Elvis
Born Free	Soundtrack	Best TV, Movie and Broadway Themes, Vol. 2
Choices	George Jones	The Cold Hard Truth
Climb Against the Odds	Climb Against the Odds	Climb Against the Odds
Climb Every Mountain	Broadway Cast	Best of Broadway
Do the Right Thing	George Strait	Blue Clear Sky
Error of Our Ways	Temptations	Emperors of Soul
Forever Young	Rod Stewart	Stars on Classic
Forgive & Forget	Avalon	A Maze of Grace
Get On Your Feet	Gloria Estefan	When You Believe - Single
God Bless the USA	Lee Greenwood	The Best of Country Gold
Hero	Mariah Carey	Here is Mariah Carey
Higher Ground	Barbara Streisand	Higher Ground
Heal the World	Michael Jackson	History
I Will Survive	Gloria Gaynor	Love Tracks
I'd Like to Teach the World to Sing	Ray Connitt	15 Most Requested Songs
If the World Had a Front Porch	Tracy Lawrence	I See it Now

40 Songs with Moral and Inspirational Messages
(continued)

Song Title	Artist	Album/CD
Imagine	John Lennon	Imagine
I'm Still Standing	Elton John	Live USA
Invincible	Pat Benetar	Synchronistic Wanderings
Lean on Me	Grover Washington, Jr.	All the King's Horses
Lessons Learned	Dan Folgelberg	Souvenirs./Netherlands
Light One Candle	Peter Yarrow	Don't Laugh at Me
Love Can Build a Bridge	The Judds	Spiritual Reflections
Never Give Up on Your Dreams	Dan Clark	I Had to Play
People	Barbara Streisand	One Voice
Put a Little Love in Your Heart	Jackie DeShannon	What the World Needs Now ...
Respect	Aretha Franklin	Aretha's Gold
Shades of Grace	Bob Carlisle	Butterfly Kisses
Some Gave All	Billy Ray Cyrus	Some Gave All
Teach Your Children	Crosby, Stills, and Nash	Daylight Again
Teaching Peace	Red Grammer	Teaching Peace
Tomorrow	Original Broadway Cast	Annie Soundtrack
Try a Little Kindness	Glen Campbell	Rhinestone Cowboy
We Are the Champions	Queen	Live in Budapest
We Are the World	USA for Africa	USA for Africa
What a Wonderful World	Louis Armstrong	What a Wonderful World
When You Believe	Whitney Houston	My Love is Your Love
You'll Never Walk Alone/I Believe	Lamelle	A Story to Tell: Hymns and Praises
You've Got to Stand for Something	Aaron Tippin	You've Got to Stand for Something